Inspired by and some credit go to

William Faulkner

Fernando Peso

Hemingway

A few Arab poets.

In forms of small stories. The author takes us into the journey in his thoughts, his feelings and what he learned through his experiences.

All stories are based on true experiences from the author's life.

"The pen and paper help us to process our emotions. It allows us to see where we went wrong, and what we could have done differently. It eases our pain and brings joy to our hearts."

A Child's Wish

When I was not myself.

I was ignoring the plain truth.

But I was contradicting myself.

And once again I ignored the plain truth.

A poet caring about the empty place.

Being tortured in this illusion.

Every time my soul flies.

A part of me gets lost.

O passersby in my memory.

Search for that child in me.

I miss being a son.

Curious, laughing, innocent troublemaker.

Life destroyed and wiped my smile.

And with tears and pain it was generous.

My sorrow became my companion.

And whenever my companion says come, I reply let us go.

My words are careful.

Yet with my silence I was not aware of what was said.

The ink is born dead in jars.

Then stays alive on papers.

"The pen and paper are the strongest expressions."

Courage

The coward dies a thousand times and the courageous dies once.

The man who said this was probably a coward.

He knew lots of things about cowards and nothing about the courageous.

The courageous if smart they die thousands of times but simply do not mention it.

I know the night is not the same as the day.

That everything is different.

That the night matters cannot be explained in the day because it gets wiped.

I know that night can be scary to courageous people when their loneliness begins.

If people possess the courage to be different or make a change.

Life will break them and if it cannot it destroys them.

Life breaks everyone.

People become stronger in these broken places.

Life destroys nice, kind, and courageous people.

If you are not one of those people, it will destroy you but there is no urgency for your turn.

The courage that I carried.

Brought the suffering upon me.

I do not possess courage anymore.

I am broken completely.

They broke me to pieces.

Like a scattered dream and a faraway memory.

Or

A scattered memory and a faraway dream.

"A scattered memory increases the courage in you."

Wrong Generation

For me to understand, I rebuilt myself.

To understand, love must be forgotten.

I no longer know a saying with a purpose and goal.

Leo da Vinci said we cannot love or hate something before we understand it.

Isolation saddens me.

Friendships conflicts me.

Having someone next to me distracts me.

Simply I enjoy dreaming about them next to me in a special way that no one usually enjoys.

The isolation imprinted on me and directed me.

Another appearance of just one person delays my thought process.

If calling someone is a relief, to me it is the opposite and not sure if the word relief can stay alive.

On my own I can be creative and produce quick answers to questions no one yet had, and with a smart and dazzling look.

This becomes different around people.

I lose the ability to explain my actions.

If I must, 15 minutes and I would be sleepy and feel nothing but sleepiness.

Yes, speaking the truth with people brings tiredness upon me and hence why I avoid it.

Only my shadowy friends of the night that I can have a real and brave conversation with.

It feels as if a soul is self-reflecting.

Which makes it heavy for me to say to someone what needs to be said upon reflection.

A simple dinner invitation is becoming nerve wrecking.

Carrying out social duties such as discussing business or waiting for someone, alone the idea of it could ruin my mood for the entire day.

Sometimes it serves as a disturbing distraction to me the whole day.

Leading to insomnia and sleeplessness at night.

When in fact reality when it happens, it is not clear, and it does not explain anything to me.

Then it happens again and repeats, and I do not learn what I was supposed to learn causing an endless cycle.

I learned my approach from being an outcast.

I do not know if Rosso or Sinclair is the one who said this "it seems these cycles the soul is always with its own reflection in its own world".

Maybe I was born in the wrong generation.

Maybe I am in a generation I cannot speak about.

"Maturing very early indeed misplaces you from your generation."

Balance

Balance, one of the most complicated concepts in this world.

Experiences introduces us to the so-called concept of balance.

Those experiences are painful and breaking.

When we stand on one leg, we lose balance after a few moments.

It causes an imbalance, and you could fall and get hurt.

We regain balance as soon as we stand back on two legs.

So, why does achieving balance takes so long?

Balance is important to every person when they become an adult.

Many fail to achieve it and some when achieved it is too late.

Most get stuck in the whirlpools that life throws at them.

Repeating the same mistakes over and over.

Trying to find that balance that they seek so much.

Acquiring balance is one of the biggest keys to happiness.

To acquire this concept that is sought by so many.

Mistakes must be done.

Mistakes that are painful and soul crushing.

Balance is more than a process.

Balance is a matter of patience.

It is a matter of time.

It is a matter of satisfaction.

A matter of influence.

A matter of surrounding people and nature.

A matter of embracement.

A matter of knowledge.

The soul might have to self-reflect millions of times.

It might have to analyze characteristics millions of times.

It might have to embrace millions of times.

It might have to gain so much knowledge.

Achieving balance is one of the greatest achievements.

Once we achieve the balance in our lives.

Our inner souls will be balanced.

Our actions will be balanced.

Only then we can find peace from within.

Only then we can live in harmony.

And most importantly.

Only then we can know and feel true happiness.

"Balance grants the harmony and happiness that we seek."

Innocent Actions

Unintentional innocent actions happen.

To protect oneself and as a survival mechanism.

In a bid to find joy and avoid pain.

These reasons lead to misunderstood actions.

That does not mean those actions are bad.

They are simply unintentional and without a moral sense.

Getting irritated of these actions is often a mistake.

It is the assumption that the person is at fault.

Mistaken to think that the person is cold hearted.

Hate lingers and the thirst for vengeance grows.

Retreating, self-reflection and the moral thought is ignored.

The wrong judgement outcome harms that person.

Instead of self-perseverance.

It is difficult to have such patience.

For someone to stop and self-reflect.

To be forgiving.

Resentment and anger are not a coping mechanism.

They are a soul breaker.

This world that is built breaks.

We attempt to fix and rebuild it.

It then breaks and collapses on top of us.

Feeling joy and avoiding pain everlasting.

That is not real.

Instead, it must be embraced.

"We must embrace happy and sad moments. It is the only way to minimize making a mistake."

Time

A story of a broken memory.

The watch broke and the arrows fell.

But the watch still sounds tick tock.

Without a care of what has happened to the arrows.

The life of this memory is just like that.

No value, no importance, and no meaning.

And time passing, exhausting itself.

It does not stop, even if it leads to nothing.

It continues to tick.

Simply numbers stay with no dedication and commitment.

Nothing is becoming of importance in life.

Everything is lost, delayed, or stuck.

Except the clock it stills ticks.

Just like the hearts and lives beating away.

And tick tock indeed.

Time passes without caring for anyone.

Without waiting for anyone.

Then there is no time to explain and give details.

Let us try to take advantage.

Let us use this time productively.

The isolations gave us the time we need.

The time that is needed to self-reflect.

To value each other, to know each other.

Because time shows you.

That no one owns it.

Time is of an essence.

We use it and win.

Or we waste it and lose.

"Time will not save you if you do not do anything to save yourself."

The Silent Humane

People are divided into two.

The silent humane and the harmful speaker.

I am part of the silent humane.

I started to seal my words.

I became aware of the beauty of ignoring.

Whereas in speaking, it is bitter.

The world is filled with beasts.

With our inner beasts.

Can you tame those beasts?

You try with kindness.

When you fail the beast tears you apart.

Our inner beasts think kindness is weakness.

Whereas we know that it is strength.

Anyone can hate.

But not everyone can be kind, forgiving and selfless.

Then other beasts try to steal your light away.

The silent actions are built and taken as a protecting
mechanism.

O my wrapped soul that is twisted.

They called it crazy when they could not figure it out.

I observed and analyzed instead of explaining.

People do not know the meaning of words.

And it hurts when they fill you with nice words that they do not mean it.

They sell you lies, and silence is better in this case.

You draw a border.

It keeps you hidden inside and locked away.

What are thoughts?

The more you pay attention to detail.

The more miserable you become.

What are we looking for?

Intentions that are honest and shown in action.

Not lies and no actions.

I had to choose between the honest and the liar.

How can I choose when I am part of the silent humane?

I must lie sometimes, to hide facts for the greater good.

The truth weight weighs heavily on my shoulder.

And that eats you away slowly.

People do not understand that because they have not experienced it or simply, they are unwilling to experience it.

In words you have to mix lies with truths.

Silence and giving no explanations when taking actions are easier.

That is why I remained silent when people are talking.

Silence does not change the truth.

However, when the truth is revealed in the correct timing it is not very painful and it does not weigh heavily on the person hearing the truth.

Protecting the truth in silence will eat you away slowly.

"To all that I hid the truth from, one day you will understand the reasons of doing so."

A Pitied Leader

Dear Human,

Greetings from your life.

Hold on, is this your life anymore?

You meet people that tell you to be yourself.

We love you as yourself.

What they mean is their image of you in their heads.

Do you notice that you slowly disintegrate to match that image?

You are often told that when you fall and stand again and that repeat it is normal.

But your heart feels quite the opposite.

They tell you to be yourself.

They are betting if they figured out where you will end up.

And they wait for that slippery slope that brings your end.

Then they say I knew this would happen.

If you go through the ramp that takes you to the sky heights.

They feel that envy and regret.

We often fear to show our kindness to not look weak.

They say these things are normal.

But that is in their lives not mine.

You live your own life.

You get exhausted looking for the right and trustworthy people.

You are the leader that is weak when it comes to yourself.

People will always conclude their own judgement whether it is real or not.

Let it be and do not try to change their outcome.

If I were like most people, I would not know that.

Because I know that I am not like most people.

I have self-awareness and individualism therefore, an outcast.

You created your own image.

Know that this huge world and life is not my responsibility.

I learned that I should be dedicated to myself.

Victory does not come on it is own.

Leaving this life that is not mine.

Going back to my own life.

Without needing to do what people expect of you.

O righteous soul do not be lost.

This world is merciless to lost souls.

When I see a lost soul.

I feel sympathy towards it.

The urge to help and guide it.

Because I understand how painful it can be.

Some glories are mine and some are others.

I am a leader that offers nothing but pity towards myself.

"Once you are leader, you end up sacrificing a lot from your life, for the benefit of your own people."

Senses And Ambitions

Everything I achieved and received too today.

I achieved it and received it with the help of my senses.

Except that I realized that our senses can fools us sometimes.

From wisdom we learn not to get comfortable with the ones that lie to us for their sake.

Even this said our senses sometimes will fools us to ignore this even if we know the truth.

Things can be beyond us.

Not understanding this will make us fall into mistakes.

We fall into them whether we were suspicious or not.

That is me covered with my grey blanket, sitting opposite of the fire in my garden holding this pen and paper.

How can I deny or delay the inevitable truth? The pen and paper are in my hands.

Here is when I remember that I am only a human.

It is in my habit to sleep and dream.

To see beyond the imagination.

So many times, I dreamt of this.

That I have reached this place.

That I have acquired that standard.

But here I am, still sleeping.

The fact that I can move my head.

Grip my hands to hold this pen and paper means that I am not sleeping.

Because in dreams this cannot happen clearly.

These ambitions have consumed me with paranoia and suspicions.

I am unable to forget them, unable to shake them and no way to get rid of them.

Just like swimming in the deep dark ocean.

It is becoming difficult to reach shore and stand on land.

It is too late now.

I have no options but to do my best to go through this path.

Moving forward, believing that I will be able to dismantle those two from myself.

It is my right to have hopes.

Even if it makes me happy, I will keep looking to find that hope.

Sometimes I wonder if I am real if what I achieved and lived is real.

People blame me for this because they do not know how I feel.

But I have the right to feel like that.

People do not know me or what I have been through.

This time I will rid myself of this paranoia.

I will rid myself of being consumed by the past.

I thought I could be completely stable.

If I were all the time, I would not be human.

I will lose myself and make mistakes between now and then.

That is what makes us humans.

My life is complicated and will only get more complicated.

I have accepted that and made peace with it.

I no longer want to spend my free time analyzing the difficulties.

I understood the risk is the difficulties that are born in my own thoughts.

"We must not obsess about our ambitions. But indeed, we must carry the passion to follow them."

An Outcast

I became an outcast for so long.

I forgot the importance of silence.

I forgot the damages words can cause.

The clouds told me that I am alone even when surrounded by people.

Because people do not understand me.

Darkness will consume you even if your hugged with love.

Sometimes even when people are around us, we still feel lonely.

It is then we have nothing but the pen and paper that takes away our loneliness.

Realizing my reality will always be hidden from others.

Those people greediness for my help grows and grows.

It tries to eat away as much as possible.

It is then, that I have no choice but to go to my own place.

It is the place where I can say what I want.

That space where there is no holding back.

The space that allows you to say the harmful words even if the truth.

And the sense of relief falls on us.

Loyalty to people have no meaning today.

I have kept my well open until people dried it up.

And I am the one left in thirst.

The night came and it asked did you base your happiness on helping and giving?

What do you think would have saved you?

A selfless helping/giving or a selfish taking?

I stayed silent for long until the pain whispered in my ears.

Saying speak and destroy with your words.

It pushed me to hate silence and patience.

It killed my brave humbleness and awoke the ugly beast in me.

Nowadays, people just talk and sell dreams and lies.

How horrible have we become?

We all want to be forgiven.

Pity and sympathy are simply not in me.

I convinced myself that I am not aware of how horrible the situation is.

I ignored the truth.

When you meet so many people it is hard to forget.

And people ignored me and my truth.

In caring for my loved ones, I was harsh.

Because of my inability to care for myself.

How did I expect fairness and loyalty from them?

O loneliness. Our minds are in harmony.

We are kind to one another.

We converse through the doors of honesty.

We see the light being taken away by darkness.

I feel it now.

Everything having it is own soul and meaning.

Everyone will want to express and aspire.

Some of my experience taught me that forgetting can be a blessing.

O loneliness, such happiness can come from you.

I hear the wind rather than listening to lies and hurtful words.

People say hurtful things and sometimes without realizing.

I learned that I must hide myself.

Hide my work.

It would have created more balance for me.

It would have reduced the hate and envy that is lingering on me from others.

And what is life?

Life is nothing but at the peak.

Feeling the breeze at the top of the mountain.

The fresh air that is entering my lungs.

Cleansing me form the toxicity that people filled me with.

This air that enlightens me.

This air that fills me with strength.

The air that makes me feel alive.

"I realized I was never alone in my life. I was alone in my ambitions and success."

Love

love is the two sides of the same coin.

It can lift you up or put you down.

Love can be self-destructing.

It can blind us from reality.

It causes us to overlook many things that hurts us.

It is that love that keep us trapped in illusions.

Love is the two sides of a coin.

It cannot be one sided.

One sided love hurts the most.

Sometimes Love causes you to let go of what you love.

You forsake your happiness for theirs.

Love is not a rose.

A rose fade quickly.

True love does not.

Love is like a tree.

It grows, falls, renews, and then grow even stronger.

Like the song.

Love lifts us up where we belong, on a mountain high.

Love is the strongest weapon there is.

It builds up the determination to keep going.

Love unleashes the infinite potential that is hidden in a person.

"Love comes in all shapes and forms. Family, friends, or partners. A special place will always be held in our hearts for our loved ones."

Life

Humans and animals.

People with high awareness feel sorry for animals.

They would feel pity of how those animals cannot express their pain.

Those people sympathize because they feel like that sometimes.

How even us humans who can speak cannot express our feelings.

It is this unbearable feeling that leads to endless fighting.

Without thinking of life's nature.

Animals are filled with blind greediness and desires.

For modernized humans, we have indeed turned into that.

What have we become to?

Attached to living life even if in a lie.

Blindly following any portrait for the sake of life itself.

Fooling themselves with false happiness.

Where did we start and where do we end up?

The more a soul is excited for life.

The more it relates to animals.

Continuing to follow their wrong desires and greediness.

That what most of us do in our lives.

The moment will come when we realize this.

We start sensing a greater being than us in the sky.

In this realization we look around frantically.

We then find the innocence that is hidden in us.

We know what sadness means.

We know what happiness means.

But there will be moments when we are forced to return to that early stage before realization.

We then need our alone time to figure out our priorities.

And what we need to do.

We stop running away and start facing it.

How did we enjoy running away from our problems just like animals?

It is like a prey running away from its predator and fails to survive.

Why do we rush in loving life, in loving wealth and in work?

With recklessness of our own lives.

We feel that is what is important than finding ourselves and our thoughts.

Is this rushing to avoid ourselves?

Pride takes over.

People do anything to show that they are happy.

When in fact they are not.

Everyone experiences that weird moment.

When we are sad, and the painful memories suddenly pours on us.

Rather than us learning to embrace it.

We try to find a way to distract us from it.

And this reveals to us that it will keep repeating.

We live fearing our memories and our emotions.

So, what is this constant worry?

What is this worry that keep us from sleeping at night?

Nature tries to tell us, but we ignore it and refuse to listen.

When we are alone and calm.

We become scared of what our thoughts will whisper in our ears.

That is why we keep ourselves occupied with spending time with people.

To avoid sitting alone with our thoughts.

What a disappointment.

From those deaf ears.

This stubborn mind and this locked heart.

What a disappointment.

When you cannot fly.

When you see something higher and cannot reach it.

When you know the way but a stone or two hinders you.

It is when one big wish comes true even if it is for one day.

Then you forget your ambitions and would like to replace them.

With that wish that came true and instead of one day for the rest of your life.

Just the thought of this isolates a person and makes them lonely.

With what words can this soul that reached this stage be described with?

It is a mysterious soul filled with kindness.

It is the soul that heals the pain.

Not like night darkness it falls. But it falls like a warm light that fills the worlds hearts.

"The pure souls pureness can be felt even when enraged."

A Heart-Warming Vision

Something shinning in the distance.

I need the holy tears to see in that distance.

The script is given.

The decision is for us.

Arguing to explain each side.

I saw a shining star.

And I asked it to guide me.

I did not sleep.

To realize a dream.

The old trees that I Shaked.

Opened and spread their arms for me.

No secret the visionary lantern told me what will happen when it saw what happened.

In the next chapter.

Sins will not be forgiven.

The pain will be a river.

Who can convince these two to not happen?

Words and meanings will come to life.

And the soul will stand at the top of the mountain.

Observing the chaos that is passing through everyone.

The wrath of the soul will then return to avenge itself.

Reality will fall on everyone very cruelly.

Even the forward-looking ones.

Will stop and look backwards.

In the next chapter.

The visions will combine and become twisted.

The roots of the fogged thoughts will grow.

And the blind will put on glasses to see through.

Instead, he will see the cruelty of the world.

Where all bad portraits and characteristics are normalized.

In the next chapter.

It will be an open auction.

Betrayals, selfishness, and greediness will be sold and bought.

I called to the clouds; I am growing weaker.

It answered. Walk through this dark map first.

And then you will see the light.

When hope dies it forces us to flip the page and begin a new chapter.

Pain, sorrow, and grief are not everlasting.

Be ready to take it out when the time comes.

Stand, pray and welcome those new souls that are calling.

Be the guiding light to those lost souls.

Let them enter from the thousand's doors of the righteous.

Let them embrace the wisdom from the pain of the
experienced.

Let them control themselves.

The future will then be green.

The light at the end of the tunnel is calling.

Open your heart and feel the warmth.

The gentle and loving warmth that falls upon us.

**"Misery is never ending but so hope is. Never lose the light
and hope in us. Hope is the thing that drives us to survive
and keep fighting."**

A Grateful Starling

Almost all different types of birds in our area descend on my garden.

They walk, they rest.

They eat and they sing.

They look me in the eye.

They do not fear me, even if I make a movement.

It is wonderful to see such birds singing in harmony.

Could it be that they are observant just like us?

Or could it be that they sense the kindness in me, or that I will not hurt them?

The fledgling starling roaming so low under the tree.

Not moving as, I approach it, refusing to fly away.

First thing comes to mind is that it is hurt.

As I approached it, it chirped and took a few steps back.

I looked down to see and realize that its loved one has died.

I took its loved one and buried it under the tree.

The fledgling still did not fly away.

It kept watching and observing my actions whilst I bury its loved one.

As I stepped back, it went standing next to the grave and stayed there without flying away.

I approached it, grabbed it, and sheltered it.

I left some food and water for it to eat and gain it is strength.

It ate and drank but still did not fly away.

It sat on my sofa embracing being by my side feeling the warm love radiating.

Then it sat on the corner and looked to the distance.

I opened the door thinking it wants to fly away.

Instead, it walked to the garden.

It walked to where its loved one was buried.

It walked back to me, stared at me, and chirped.

It then flew away.

That is when I understood the bird was not physically hurt.

It was mourning the death of its loved one.

Roaming around its loved one's scent.

It could not eat whilst processing its loss.

Once its loved one was buried, it ate and regained strength.

It was able to stay its farewell to its loved one and let nature take its course.

It wanted its loved one to be resting in peace. Seeing the burial made it real.

It embraced being my side and regaining the strength.

I felt that it was thanking me for helping it when it stared and chirped at me.

Saying it is farewells and letting go, the fledgling starling flew away.

What a relief, what a fascinating feeling.

The gentle loving warmth that I felt.

We indeed are not alone in this world.

Humans, even animals suffer from losses.

We all need some time to process our loss.

It is just that we must embrace it and learn to let go when the time comes.

We do not have to always show our appreciation with words.

We can also show it by actions.

Just like the fledgling starling showed me without speaking.

We must express our appreciation to our loved ones before it is too late.

"Processing anything takes time. We must make the time to process it to be able to let go."

True friendships

True friendships

Sometimes we can be ungrateful and unappreciative when we have a valuable friend.

I learned that from spending time with many different people.

I learned that from failing to appreciate who I have by my side.

Once you achieve and gain much, you get lost and forget to appreciate it.

The absence of certain people in our lives can be a blessing.

It opens our eyes to how good things were when this friend was part of our lives.

When there are good friends that are helping us, we get used to it.

We easily get used to how easy things become.

How smoother and lovely our life becomes.

To know that you can rely on someone in your time of need.

It is a huge sense of relief that befalls on us.

When we get used to it, it becomes difficult to distinguish the good parts without them.

We fail to understand how lucky to have such friends or family by our side.

When we realize that it becomes a sorrowful memory.

Because we wish if we have composed ourselves.

If we have done right by those friends.

We wish if we have not lost them or hurt them.

We have a saying that goes "far from the eye, far from the heart".

I do not believe in that at all.

No matter the distance true friends will always have that bond.

When they meet after a long time, they can sit comfortably and smile next to each other.

There are different levels of friends.

Those who lead a busy life and those who lead a simple life.

You have friends that can help much more than you can help them yourself.

Friends that are on a different level of maturity, success, and kindness.

Those friends that give time priority to you.

Those who won't let you down.

Those who you can always go to.

Then you have friends that only look after themselves.

The ones that will not appreciate how much you do for them.

The ones that will return the least amount towards you.

Those that blame you for their mistakes and those that they say helping us was a choice.

It is unfortunate that we indeed have reached a time where true friends are something rare to come by.

It is this time where pride takes over.

Where friends cannot admit their mistakes and apologize.

Where they keep resenting each other rather than forgiving and learning from each other.

Friends are on different levels.

Those that are selfless, and kind are rare.

Those that want to be your friend and those that need you in their life for their advantage.

Wanting and needing a friend is a completely different thing.

In the end, we always manage to see the friends that have the courage to say sorry.

The friends that try to be better.

The friends that are there in happy and sad moments.

Those that are loyal.

Having a true friendship is indeed becoming of a rarity in this modern age.

"We must appreciate the friends that gives us more than we can ever return. We must show how grateful we are or having them before it is too late."

Satisfaction, Stability And Happiness

We are unable to know where happiness is until a certain time in our lives.

In every generation, the ages 15-22 are lost.

Yet no one can figure out their thought process.

Every generation's environment is different, so their thought process is different.

We often forget that. We forget to offer them guidance.

Guidance should be made available but not to push for an outcome.

It is to keep the options open.

This age is lost because we are not given the options.

Instead, we are pushed to different paths.

The paths that our parents want.

The paths that the schools draw for us.

The path that makes us happy.

At this age, we lack the understanding of what happiness means.

I learned that happiness is in life stability.

When you have the balance.

When you can take a day off without having to worry about an expense.

To achieve happiness, we must know what is right and wrong.

Happiness is something that is worked for.

We must find our passion.

We must set our ambitions.

We must live, dream, learn and thrive.

Once we live in the right way.

We can dream.

Once we have a dream.

We can learn.

Once we learn.

We thrive.

Once we thrive, we learn what stability is.

Life stability is significant when seeking happiness.

Stable in living, in work, and in mind.

No matter the strength of the storm we can always survive if we are on a stable footing.

We can always be happy.

Stability can be gained only when we are satisfied with what we have.

We are satisfied with the things in our life.

Without wanting or demanding more.

Appreciating the things in our life.

Thinking of necessities rather than commodities.

Having materialistic stuff is not happiness, it is greediness.

It is the obsession of wanting more.

Let's be satisfied with what we have.

Let's find our life stability.

Then we find our way.

We find our way to happiness.

"Happiness only comes when you accept your challenges, rather than complaining and avoiding them."

Knowledge

Knowledge is power.

Knowledge can open all the doors to success.

Humans born in the past, born now, or yet to be born will acquire different knowledge.

Knowledge changes every decade, century, and generation.

We learn and acquire that knowledge to protect ourselves.

To take care of our loved ones, to pursue our dreams, ambitions and to succeed.

Like everything, knowledge can also be destructive.

The more we learn, the more curious we get.

No matter how much we know we still want to know more.

Forgetting can be a blessing. Once you know something you cannot forget it.

Knowing can be hurtful. Sometimes it is best not to know things.

Knowing things or the truth at the wrong time can be painful.

Knowledge can take us to places but it can isolate us and brings misery.

When you acquire lots of knowledge, it becomes difficult to have conversations with people.

The level of knowledge will be higher than many people.

You end up having to explain a lot.

People around you will not be on your level.

They will not be able to advise you or help you because they lack the knowledge of how to do so.

It becomes increasingly difficult to find people to assist you to progress.

The knowledge that I acquired changed the world around me.

It made me get older and wrinkly before my age.

The more knowledge you acquire the more bored you become.

It will make you want to stay on the move to do new things.

Knowing that there will always be more than what the eye sees.

It is then chasing for more what makes you feel alive.

To see the new things and learn the new things.

Remembering when I used to be a child.

Not realizing that I am living in the same routine.

Getting excited to do the same thing over and over.

When we forget quickly and easily.

Forgetting can be a blessing. I learned that the hard way.

Forgetting can sometimes make us happy. Just like when we were children.

Sometimes I wish that I did not acquire this knowledge.

This knowledge opened the pandora box of the grey area.

Being trapped in this area is easy.

Leaving that area is very difficult.

It is that grey area that has unlimited possibilities.

It is that area that strains your brain to analyze the possibilities.

Overworking your brain to make the correct decision.

It is the area that makes you fear the unknown.

I used that knowledge as much as I can.

Fearing the unknown.

I created the future. The future I wanted to see.

But I have failed to understand things can be beyond us.

We must face our fears even if it means entering the unknown.

Rather than avoiding, we should be prepared to stand firm to whatever it brings.

Because we have the knowledge that is necessary to be able to adapt.

"We must not dwell on every detail because of the knowledge we have. The more we think about it, the more difficulties arise".

A Second Chance

When you get another chance at life, it should not go to waste.

You have to take care of yourself. To use all your strength.

To live and invest to the fullest.

I will not say everything I want.

I will definitely think about everything I am going to say.

I will value everything that deserves value.

I will dedicate the time for myself and for my loved ones.

I will continue to sleep and dream.

We see the lights when we open our eyes.

We see the darkness when we close our eyes.

The same thing goes for life.

There are moments of darkness.

But there are moments of light.

Death comes in all ways not just from old age.

When we get another chance, we should aim for the mountain heights.

I will continue my way. I will walk in the path that I believe to be right.

I will be awake when everyone sleeping.

I will return to my glory and be better than before.

I will live, care, dedicate things to myself.

There are no guarantees in life.

The older we get.

The more we get attached to life.

Not knowing how many days we have left.

Wanting to live it to the fullest.

The reason flowers are beautiful is because their blinding beauty does not last.

The same goes for our lives.

Live today like there is no tomorrow.

And think for tomorrow like life is forever lasting.

Do not wait at all.

Do what you must.

Express what needs to be expressed.

Pass on what needs to be passed on.

Appreciate the people you have and what you have.

Be there for your loved ones.

Even if there is tomorrow.

We must continue to do so.

It is a chance for us to redeem ourselves.

A chance for us to become and to do better.

Encourage people to dream and support them.

Take all the time you need to put on a smile.

Say you understand.

Say forgive me.

Say I forgive you.

Say excuse, I am sorry, and thank you.

Because before you know it. It will be too late.

Regret won't do a thing then.

"I am sorry to everyone that I hurt or harmed. Forgive me and excuse me for my mistakes. To everyone that harmed me or hurt me, I forgive you."

Memories

We cultivate so many memories in our lives.

Those memories keep us alive.

Those memories teach us and remind us of our actions.

You travel, you see new things.

You meet new people; you make friends and enemies.

It is indeed tiring to cultivate memories with people that will no longer be part of your life.

Even friends can leave you one day or betray you.

Day pass and nothing will remain but these memories.

Having many memories with different people can be scary.

It is when you remember that friend or that person that is no longer part of your life.

It is that happy memory that makes you think and ask how did things go wrong?

My brain has stored many memories of almost all types of lives, people, friends, and enemies.

Until the day that it was broken and scattered.

My memories became of no meaning.

But those memories bring upon you the nostalgic feeling.

When you feel happy and sad at the same time.

Happy for that lovely memory and sad for knowing this memory won't be repeated.

It is then that I understood memories are just like life.

Every memory has a meaning.

Memories develop our feelings, actions, and personalities.

Memories are simply our experiences of the past.

What type of thing can be a part of a person without a memory?

Without memory, we are just lost.

How many times the thought of life being just a big dream occurs?

We then think of the greater being in the sky that is watching over us.

Looking at the fascinating sky and the stars that fills it.

Looking at it gives us a sense of hope.

We all experience that moment when we suddenly look to the sky.

We then remember a happy moment instantly no matter how far in the past.

We feel the regaining of our strength.

Giving us the hope to keep dreaming.

It is those memories that help us to understand things we could not understand in the past.

It is then we remember something good and wish that we had the patience.

We then say perhaps things could have worked out.

Those memories that keep replaying in my head bringing sadness to my heart.

That is the mirror that shows me my face and appearance.

The way my face change and look different but then returns to its old self.

Just like those memories.

It is those memories that are embraced with time, and we learn to live with them.

We kiss grief goodbye, and the happy memories are the ones to stay alive in us.

Indeed, I kissed the grief goodbye and now I cannot stop smiling remembering those lovely memories.

"Memories drive us, keeps our conscience alive. Whatever the memory was let's embrace it and remember it and smile."

Caring

In caring for my loved ones, I was harsh.

Because of my inability to care for me.

I have reached a stage that I have the resources and capability to help.

When it comes to the people I care about, I went beyond.

I cared and helped unconditionally.

No one was able to help or care for me the same way.

When I care for someone, I do not expect anything in return.

Seeing the smiles on their faces is a reward enough for me.

Those people that you care for hurt you in the end.

Caring deteriorates a soul slowly.

You care for your people and forget to care for yourself.

Can you blame me?

I was able to give much more than them.

I had the resources, the ability, and the capacity to easily do so.

I learned that I should be dedicated to myself.

The people that I cared for brought suffering and pain upon me.

I stood firm regardless of my own troubles for their sake.

I could not go away or look after myself.

They needed me. All of them.

I rushed into helping each one of them.

I ensured that whatever is done for them won't go to waste.

I ensured that they stay on their feet regardless of how horrible their situation is.

I succeeded and protected all.

There was the thought of not being able to do so myself.

In that thought, I created a system.

To keep an eye from far on the people that I care about.

To intervene and protect them when necessary.

In doing so, I was successful.

However, unexpected tragedy hit the world.

An invisible enemy hit the world.

I started to lose my resources.

To lose everything I worked for.

My life that I spent the last 5 years building.

Sleeping 3-4 hours a day.

I had to be the strong one for them.

Parts of me died slowly to be their strength.

Difficult as it comes, you cannot just stand by and not do anything.

Especially when it comes to the people you care about.

We can look down on people.

But only when we are opening our hands to lift them up.

We open our hands until we bring them to land, and they can stand.

They kept on needing more. No one could see how weak I became.

I stood firm and they kept on asking for more thinking I am still strong.

Slowly I lost control. I started losing what I have.

My health decreased, my strength everything went sideways.

At that moment I lost myself and I became outraged.

I started being harsh on the ones that I cared about.

Implementing whatever is needed for them to stay on their feet.

Even if I had to force it earlier than it should have been.

Even if they did not appreciate it now. They will understand it later.

Doing so knowing that my days of being able to be there for them are limited.

Sometimes you simply cannot turn your back on people that need help.

Imagine the people you care about; you could never turn your back on them.

I failed those that I care about. The people that believed in me.

I fell and I stood, and it repeated over and over.

The day came where I could not stand anymore.

It is then I understood that I failed myself.

No one was willing to stop me.

No one was willing to go that extra step to use the means to stop me.

When it comes to the people I care about. My potential is infinite.

I can keep going until the last second.

No one had the potential or the willingness to keep their efforts into stopping me.

I have reached a place where I cannot be recovered easily.

My recovery is going to take a long time.

I learned that no one deserves that level of care.

Caring has indeed deteriorated me slowly.

The quality that I cannot change and cannot get rid of.

The question is will I be able to stop myself in the future?

"To all my loved ones, the ones that left to a better place, the ones that are part of my life and the ones that I failed. When you feel alone and sad, remember that my soul will always be watching over you."

The Author

MOHAMAD AL AMRY

25/12/1999

CEO OF HORIZON MAB LIMITED

HORIZONLIMITED.CO.UK

CHAIRMAN OF THE UAE-UK FREINDSHIP FORUM

UK-UAE-FRIENDSHIPFORUM.CO.UK

"Do not wait for the future. Work hard and create the future you want to see".

Authors Bio

Mohamad Al Amry is the founder of Horizon MAB Limited. An innovative investment firm specializing in Legal, Education and Tourism, Catering and Technology. He founded Horizon MAB Limited which has multiple branches globally and its HQ is based in London, England. Mohamad has vast experience working externally with police forces. He is a former member of the Metropolitan Special Constabulary and has a robust and varied educational background stemming from his days in the U.A.E and UK. He has qualifications in primary / secondary teaching, sports leadership, electronics, electricals, childcare, spectator safety, pediatrics nursing, first aid and safety officer. He gained a bachelor's degree in politics and international relations from Queen Mary University London.

Mohamad's scholarly prowess is best represented in his stint as the student president of Uxbridge college 2017/18, where under his stewardship the students were able to eliminate their hurdles and progress. He was also a sitting member of the 13 Governors at Uxbridge College 2017/18 where his work allowed to the college to develop and improve. He has an active role in supporting the UK government. Campaigning, Volunteering, advising, and working with the UK Cabinet Ministers since 2016. Additionally, he ran for council elections in London in 2018.

Mohamad has overcome many struggles and hurdles, becoming a remarkable success and an inspiration to many on a national and global scale.